TAKING CHARGE OF YOUR FUTURE

TRANSITIONAL PREPARATION AND PLANNING GUIDE

GERALD BRADFORD, TERRENCE MORGAN, FRANKLYN SMITH

Taking Charge of Your Future: Transitional Preparation and Planning Guide
Second Edition Trade Book, 2022
Copyright © 2022 Gerald Bradford, Terrence Morgan, Franklyn Smith

All rights reserved. No part of this publication may be reproduced, stored in a retrieval system, or transmitted in any form by any means—electronic, mechanical, photocopy, recording, or otherwise—except for brief quotations in critical reviews or articles, without the prior permission of the publisher, except as provided by U.S. copyright law.

To order additional books:
www.freshstartps.org

ISBN: 978-1-952943-14-0
Editorial and Book Packaging: Inspira Literary Solutions, Gig Harbor, WA
Printed in the USA

*"Every great dream begins with a dreamer.
Always remember, that within you are the strength, patience,
and passion to reach for the stars and bring change to the world!"
-Harriet Tubman*

TABLE OF CONTENTS

Introduction	1
Note to Facilitators	3
MODULE 1: Why You Need a Plan	9
MODULE 2: Who Am I?	11
MODULE 3: Influences of Social Media and Music	13
MODULE 4: What Is a Belief?	16
MODULE 5: Values and Vices	19
MODULE 6: The Four Basic Styles of Communication	24
MODULE 7: What Is a Productive Relationship?	27
MODULE 8: What Does Success Mean to You?	29
MODULE 9: Barriers to Success	31
MODULE 10: Relapse Prevention	33
MODULE 11: Your Support Network	36
MODULE 12: Your Personal-Centered Plan	40
MODULE 13: Goals, Positive Activities, and Perspective	50
MODULE 14: Dealing with Transition	55
MODULE 15: Career Assessment	58
MODULE 16: Financial Management and Budgeting	65
MODULE 17: Developing Your Transition Plan	67
MODULE 18: Your 30-Day Goals	74
MODULE 19: Your Six-Month Goals	76
MODULE 20: Your One-Year Goals	78
MODULE 21: Your Three-Year Goals	80
Conclusion	83
About the Authors	85

INTRODUCTION

No successful business, person, or organization has achieved success without having a plan of action outlining *what* and *how* they were going to achieve their desired goals. Having a plan is simply a part of success—in every area of life.

An individualized transition plan is a written pathway that can serve as a personalized blueprint for achieving future objectives. This workbook has been created as a tool in your toolkit to assist as you develop your personal transition plan, and also as a way of introducing you to the power of self-knowledge. Our goal is to help you understand how to unlock the true potential of your ability to create the lifestyle you desire for yourself and your family.

This workbook is divided into 20 impactful modules that will help you reconnect with yourself—identifying your goals, strengths, and weaknesses, as well as the internal and external barriers that may be preventing you from achieving your goals. We are sure that by the time you complete this workbook, you will become more aware of yourself and have more confidence in your ability to start living a quality, productive, positive life.

The most beautiful aspect of self-knowledge is the personal empowerment you will feel once you begin to realize that the life you desire is within your own grasp. You just need to harness your own strength, understand how to address your weaknesses, and develop your transition plan.

So, let's get started!

NOTE TO FACILITATORS

Thank you for your participation in the vital work of helping individuals who are looking for a "fresh start" in their lives. The Fresh Start PS Organization and the *Taking Charge of Your Future* course offer an opportunity to create a clean slate.

The 20 modules in the *Taking Charge of Your Future* manual are designed to be used interactively with participants, either in a one-on-one or a group setting. The course can be self-paced or set up on a schedule (e.g., once a week, bi-weekly, etc.), as desired. We suggest allowing participants time to respond to the prompts and questions in each module on their own, and then discussing their responses during meeting times.

Module 11, in particular, requires some extra preparation on the part of the facilitator:

Person-centered planning (PCP) is an interactive interview between participants. You, the facilitator, should have already prepared your own PCP. If not, you may use an existing PCP that is reflective of the participant's life experience.

If you are working with a group, the students should be divided into groups of two; if there is an odd number of participants, the facilitator should work with the student that was left out of the pairing. Try to have students work with someone whom they do not already know. Once students are paired up, have them sign their name on the first page of their PCP plan ("_____'s Places). Have students exchange their books with each other. Now each student should have their partner's PCP.

Each person should write their partner's name at the top of the rest of the pages in this exercise (Places, Choices, etc.). Participants will be interviewing one another for the whole of this exercise and recording one another's answers in the spaces provided.

The facilitator PCP should be working from a completed PCP they can use to illustrate and explain. Try to use a PCP that is appropriate to the age of the group or individual with whom you are working . If you are using this exercise with young people, use a PCP that is written from a young person's point of view. If you are using this exercise for adults, please use a PCP reflective of an older adult's view point.

When facilitating person-centered planning in person, if available, use large, white sheets of paper, or a whiteboard, to draw PCP Places, People, Circles, lists of Likes and Dislikes, Strengths/Talents, Choices, Fears/Worries, Dreams, and finally, the Action Plan, for the whole group to see.

Places

The facilitator should share their PCP Places by drawing three concentric circles on the large, white paper or whiteboard (use the example from Module 11 on page 30). Think of the circles as a target with a bullseye: the center is where you spend the most time, the second ring identifies locations you frequent sometimes, and the outer ring is where you go occasionally. For example, participants might include: Center ring—home, second ring—school/work, third ring—friends' houses (specify). Please make sure to encourage participants to really think about where they spend their time.

The facilitator should share the example (or his/her own) wheel with participants, then have the students interview each other and record their partner's responses.

When the students have completed the activity, ask them to turn the page and write their partner's name on the on the top of the next page.

People

Next, share your sample diagram of "PCP People" by drawing three circles (use the example from the workbook on page 31). The middle circle identifies people with whom you spend the most time, the middle circle is people with whom you *frequently* spend time, and the outer circle is people with whom you *sometimes/occasionally* spend time.

For example: center ring—mother/father, brothers, sisters, etc., second ring—friends (be specific), third ring—people with whom you sometimes associate (e.g., coaches, teachers, mentors, extended family). Please make sure to encourage participants to really think about the people with whom they spend their time.

Once you've shared your wheel with participants, have them interview each other and record their partner's responses. When the students have completed the activity, ask them to turn the page and write their partner's name on the top of the next page.

NOTE TO FACILITATORS

Like and Dislikes

Share examples of what a participant might list for likes and dislikes:

Likes: learning, reading, fishing, making friends
Dislikes: two-faced people, dishonest people, politics

For this exercise, you should share your own likes and dislikes (or those on your sample exercise, if it's not your own) as a list. Once the facilitator shares their Likes and Dislikes list with participants, have students interview each other and record their partner's responses.

When the students have completed the activity, ask them to turn the page and write their partner's name on the top of the next page.

Strengths and Talents

Share examples of what a participant might list for strengths/talents: music, speaking, basketball, football, acting, speaking different languages, etc.

Similar to the Likes and Dislikes list above, share the list of your own strengths and talents (or those on the sample you are using) with the participant(s). Once the facilitator shares their Strengths and Talents list with participants, have them interview each other and record their partner's responses. When the students have completed the activity, ask them to turn the page and write their partner's name on the top of the next page.

Choices

In this exercise, participants are being asked to share their choices about things like attending school, going to work, working out, eating healthy food, and having positive friends, etc.

You, the facilitator, should share your own list of PCP Choices, or those on the example PCP you are using. Once you've shared your Choices list with participants, have students interview each other and record their partner's responses.

When the students have completed the activity, ask them to turn the page and write their partner's name on the top of the next page.

Fears/Worries

Examples of what a participant might list for fears/worries: death, police, not having enough money to live, "How will I be able to pay the rent?"

You, the facilitator, should share your own Fears and Worries list, or those on the example PCP you are using. Once you've shared your list with participants, have students interview each other and record their partner's responses.

When the students have completed the activity, ask them to turn the page and write their partner's name on the top of the next page.

Dreams

Ask participants to identify an aspirational dream (or dreams) related to at least one of these subjects: education, family/home life, employment, clean and sober living, etc.

Again, share your own PCP Dreams, or those on your example, as a list. This step is particularly important. Specify that they should list outs dreams for which they can develop an action plan to achieve.

Once you've shared your own Dreams List (or example) with participants, have students interview each other and record their partner's responses.

When the students have completed the activity, ask them to return their partner's PCP Dreams List. Once the original owner has their list, ask them to number the PCP with their most important dream being number 1 on the list.

Action Plan

In some ways, an action plan is a "heroic" act: it helps us turn our dreams into a reality. An action plan is a way to make sure your vision is made concrete. It describes the way you will use its strategies to meet its objectives. An action plan consists of a number of action steps or changes to be brought about in your community.

Each action step or change to be sought should include the following information:

- ▸ **What** actions or changes will occur
- ▸ **Who** will carry out these changes
- ▸ **By when** they will take place, and for how long

NOTE TO FACILITATORS

- **What resources** (e.g., money, staff) are needed to carry out these changes
- **Status** (Active of pending action)

Encourage participants to revisit their Action Plan bi-weekly in order to gauge progress.

Final Words

The *Taking Charge of Your Future* workbook is intended to be a "take-away" journal that the participant can keep and refer to in the months and years to come as a reminder and accountability tool. Encourage students to hang onto these books, and to remember that each day is a new day, and a new opportunity for a "fresh start"!

MODULE 1

Why You Need a Plan

There are many benefits to implementing a Personal Strategy Plan in your life. Here is a list of those benefits (though not exhaustive), and the positive effect they will have on your life and future success.

A Personal Strategy Plan can:

- help you stay on track to reaching your SMART (Specific, Measurable, Achievable, and Timely) Goals
- be helpful in finding resources and new opportunities to assist you in achieving your goals
- be used as a personal business and/or life plan for you and your family to follow
- reduce the internal stress associated with making life-changing choices
- improve your confidence and reduce the probability of returning to negative thinking, an unhealthy lifestyle, and the court system
- make you aware of the community support groups available for support, encouragement, and accountability
- provide structure to help you keep up with your daily routine
- help you to create backup Plans B, C, and sometimes D
- help you to be organized and prepared for all situations
- help you identify and assess obstacles you may have to face down the road
- make you aware of other types of community resources available to you (food, clothing, shelter, financial aid, hot meals, etc.)
- be useful in helping you articulate and communicate your plan with other family members and your support network

TAKING CHARGE OF YOUR FUTURE

Creating a strategy plan will take some effort on your part. Do what you can and be honest with what you can accomplish on your own. Let your friends and associates know what you are trying to accomplish and ask for HELP if needed! You are not meant to do this on your own.

If you do not utilize your plan, then it cannot help you get where you want to go in life. Be diligent about using it. Eventually, it will become second nature. There is nothing to lose and everything to gain by creating your Personal Strategy Plan and implementing it in your life!

What are your thoughts about developing a Personal Strategy Plan? What parts seem exciting to you; what parts intimidate you?

_____

_____

_____

_____

_____

_____

_____

_____

_____

_____

MODULE 2

Who Am I?

Part of being able to move forward in life is the ability to look back at where you're coming from. In your own words, how have you seen yourself change? How would you *like* to change? You can have the confidence to know that you have the answers within you.

These questions will help you with some self-identification and self-awareness:

What kind of person have you been in the past?

___

___

___

___

What kind of person are you today?

___

___

___

___

TAKING CHARGE OF YOUR FUTURE

Is there a change? Why and how?

_____
_____
_____
_____

What kind of person do you want to be?

_____
_____
_____
_____

How do you want to be remembered?

_____
_____
_____
_____

MODULE 3

The Effects of Social Media and Music

As human beings, we receive information from three basic sources: family (immediate and extended), community (schools, churches, clubs, etc.), and media (social media, TV, music, videos, etc.). This exercise is to help you identify how social media—as well as music—can influence our attitudes, beliefs, and choices (ABCs) in a positive or negative way. For example, how do these things influence the way we dress? Or the type of people we are attracted to? Or our everyday lifestyle choices?

Please describe how much time you spend on social media on any given day.

_____

_____

_____

_____

List four impacts/influences that social media has had on you in a positive way.

_____

_____

_____

_____

TAKING CHARGE OF YOUR FUTURE

List four impacts/influences that social media has had on you in a negative way.

_____

_____

_____

_____

What music/song best describes you? Why?

_____

_____

_____

_____

How does social media and/or certain genres of music make you feel? Please identify your feelings (positive or negative) when you are utilizing these.

_____

_____

_____

_____

MODULE 3

What are some productive things you can do as a substitute for using social media?

_____

_____

_____

_____

How do you think social media, or certain genres of music, can influence a person's attitude, beliefs, and choices?

_____

_____

_____

_____

MODULE 4

What Is a Belief?

Our actions, attitudes, and behaviors are dictated by what we believe and what we value.

> **Definition of "BELIEF"**
>
> A state or habit of mind in which trust and confidence are placed in a person or thing (i.e., belief in God, belief in democracy, etc.)
>
> ▶ acceptance that a statement is true
> ▶ acceptance that something exists
> ▶ a firmly held opinion or conviction

In this exercise, based on your values, please identify three positive activities or behaviors that you will engage in, going forward.

1. _____

2. _____

3. _____

MODULE 4

List three of your most strongly-held beliefs:

Belief 1: _____

Belief 2: _____

Belief 3: _____

Why are your top three beliefs important to you?

_____

_____

_____

_____

Why do you value each of them?

_____

_____

_____

_____

TAKING CHARGE OF YOUR FUTURE

How can your beliefs be a barrier or an obstacle on your journey to success?

_____

_____

_____

_____

What are some beliefs that can be beneficial in achieving your goals?

_____

_____

_____

_____

What are some things we need to remember about our beliefs?

_____

_____

_____

_____

MODULE 5

Values and Vices

> **Definition of "VALUE"**
> 1. A principal or ideal that is intrinsically valuable or desirable
> 2. An essential standard that inclines one to act or choose to act in one way or another

In this exercise, please think about three different things (people, places, objects) that you value in your life. What are they?

Value 1: _____

Value 2: _____

Value 3: _____

Why are your top three values important to you?

_____

_____

TAKING CHARGE OF YOUR FUTURE

Why do you value them?

_____

_____

_____

How can your values be a barrier or obstacle on your road to success?

_____

_____

_____

What are some values that can be beneficial in achieving your goals?

_____

_____

_____

What are some things we need to remember about our values?

_____

_____

_____

MODULE 5

NOTE: Your values will be demonstrated by your priorities. Where you spend the majority of your time (priorities) reflects what you value. Someone may say, "I value my family," but spends most of their time elsewhere. This begs the question, what do they *actually* value?

In the case of an adult who says they value their family, but in reality, spends most of their time at the bar, drinking with friends, their priority reflects their actually value (drinking, not family), and in this case is actually demonstrating a *vice*.

Our vices are another part of our personalities and lifestyles that will dictate how we act and other decisions we make about our lives. Being honest and self-aware about what these issues are for each of us is the first step to overcoming them.

Based on your past behavior, what are three vices you tend to engage in that lead to negative behavior and/or outcomes?

1. _____

2. _____

3. _____

Definition of "VICE"

1. An immoral or bad habit or practice
2. Immoral conduct; derived or degrading behavior

In this exercise, please describe what behaviors you have displayed in the past that were linked to your top vices.

_____

_____

_____

How can your vices be an obstacle or barrier on your road to success?

_____

_____

_____

What are some vices that can be beneficial in achieving your goals?

_____

_____

_____

What are some points we need to remember about our vices?

_____

_____

_____

Things to Consider

Keep these pieces of information in mind as you continue to work through your transition and toward independence and success:

- All our behaviors are linked to our most-deeply held beliefs. Our VALUES determine our BEHAVIORS.
- Some beliefs are linked to culture and the way we were raised. These beliefs may have had value during that period, but now need to be re-examined to see if they still apply to our current circumstances.

MODULE 5

- Some beliefs are based on emotions, not logic, so they are often wrong and unhelpful to our success.
- Negative beliefs lead to negative values, which in turn lead to negative behavior.
- Knowing your beliefs and values helps you know yourself on a deeper level, which in turn lets you control your life.
- Your values will be demonstrated by your priorities. Where you spend the majority of your time (priorities) reflects what you value. Someone may say, "I value my family," but spends most of their time elsewhere. Whatever that other priority is tells you what they *actually* value.
- Most people believe that by identifying the major triggers (people, places, media, substances) that influence negative behaviors, they will be okay. But in doing so, it's easy to overlook the minor issues in their life that set the stage for the major issues to happen.
- By becoming aware of the minor issues, you will be able to avoid the traps that lead to a destructive lifestyle.

MODULE 6

The Four Basic Styles of Communication

Passive ▶ Aggressive ▶ Passive-Aggressive ▶ Assertive

Most conflicts, whether they are professional or personal, are usually the product of some type of unmet need. If we are unable to articulate (communicate) what the unmet need is, then we can never achieve a positive result that will satisfy the underlying issue.

An effective, positive, and professional communicator is one who has developed an understanding of the four basic types of communication styles described below. In this exercise, you will assess which of the four basic styles of communication relates to you. You'll also identify why you believe you are that type of communicator, and which styles of communication you prefer others use when speaking to you.

Passive Communication:

- Individuals develop a pattern of avoiding expressing their opinions or feelings, protecting their rights, and identifying and meeting their needs.
- These individuals do not respond openly to hurtful or anger-inducing situations.
- They instead unknowingly allow grievances and annoyances to build up.
- Once their high tolerance threshold for unacceptable behavior has been reached, they are prone to explosive outbursts, which usually seem out of proportion to the triggering incident.
- They then may return to their passive state after the outburst due to feeling shame, guilt, or confusion.

Common Behaviors of Passive Communicators:

- Failing to assert or advocate for themselves
- Allowing others to purposely or unintentionally infringe on their rights
- Failing to express their feelings, needs, or opinions
- Tending to speak softly or apologetically
- Exhibiting poor eye contact and slumped body posture

Aggressive Communication:

- Individuals express their feelings and opinions and advocate for their needs in a way that violates the rights of others. Thus, aggressive communicators are verbally and/or physically abusive.

Common Behaviors of Aggressive Communicators:

- Trying to dominate others
- Using humiliation to control others
- Criticizing, blaming, or attacking others
- Being very impulsive
- Having low frustration tolerance
- Speaking in a loud, demanding, and overbearing voice
- Acting threateningly and rudely
- Not listening well
- Interrupting frequently
- Using "you" statements
- Having an overbearing or intimidating posture

Passive-Aggressive Communication:

- Individuals appear passive on the surface but are really acting out anger in a subtle, indirect, or behind-the-scenes way. These individuals usually feel powerless, stuck, and resentful. They feel incapable of dealing directly with the object of their resentments. Instead, they express their anger by undermining the object (real or imagined) of their resentments.

Common Behaviors of Passive-Aggressive Communicators:

- Muttering to themselves rather than confronting the person or issue
- Having difficulty acknowledging their anger
- Using facial expressions that don't match how they feel (like smiling when angry)
- Using sarcasm
- Denying there is a problem
- Appearing cooperative while purposely doing things to annoy and disrupt
- Using subtle sabotage to get even

Assertive Communication:

- Individuals clearly state their opinions and feelings, and firmly advocate for their rights and needs without violating the rights of others. These individuals value themselves, their time, and their emotional, spiritual, and physical needs and are strong advocates for themselves while being very respectful of the rights of others.

Common Traits of Assertive Communicators:

- They feel connected to others.
- They feel in control of their lives.
- They can mature because they address issues and problems as they arise.
- They create a respectful environment for others to grow and mature.

Now do a self-assessment:

1. Which style of communication best describes you?

_____

2. Why do you believe you are that kind of communicator?

_____

3. Which style(s) of communication would you prefer others use when speaking with you? Why?

_____

MODULE 7

What Is a Productive Relationship?

A "productive relationship" is defined as a **partnership that achieves desired outcomes**. Have you ever been in a relationship where you and another person have achieved a positive outcome? Was the relationship edifying, meaning you brought out the best in each other?

In this exercise, please list some individuals (family, friends, co-workers, etc.) with whom you have had a productive relationship:

_____

_____

_____

_____

_____

_____

TAKING CHARGE OF YOUR FUTURE

What do you need for a productive relationship?

_____

_____

_____

_____

_____

_____

MODULE 8

What Does Success Mean to You?

Success—the opposite of failure—is defined as the status of having achieved and accomplished a specific aim or objective. Being successful means that you have achieved your desired visions and goals.

In this exercise you will provide examples of things that you would like to accomplish and then identify what barriers may be preventing you from achieving them. Once your barriers are identified, you can develop a plan for overcoming them.

1. _____

2. _____

3. _____

4. _____

5. _____

What are the barriers holding you back from your success?

1. _____

2. _____

TAKING CHARGE OF YOUR FUTURE

3. _____

4. _____

5. _____

MODULE 9

Barriers to Success

Fear.

Fear is defined as an unpleasant emotion caused by the belief that someone or something is dangerous, likely to cause pain, or a threat. Fear of success becomes a barrier when we start to believe the negative comments of others, as well as our own negative self-talk, that tells us we will never accomplish our goals. Comments like "You're not good enough," or, "You'll never stay out of trouble," or, "You'll never amount to anything," can trap us in fear. Don't let the acronym of the word FEAR (False-Evidence-Appearing-Real) stop you from reaching your goals and realizing the successful and fulfilling life you deserve!

In this exercise, please answer the following questions about how you have allowed your fears to hold you back:

What is the one fear that you feel has been holding you back the most?

What have you done to remove that barrier from your life?

_____

_____

_____

TAKING CHARGE OF YOUR FUTURE

Name four other fears that you have:

1. _____

2. _____

3. _____

4. _____

What are the three things you would most like to remove from your life?

1. _____

2. _____

3. _____

What are the three things you would most like to include in your life?

1. _____

2. _____

3. _____

MODULE 10

Relapse Prevention

"Failure to plan is planning to fail."

We do not always know what is going to happen. However, when we look at an uncertain future, we can make plans for what we would do in general situations as a way of preparing. It is always helpful to have an idea of how you would react in "what if" situations. Preparation and proper planning lead to success.

In this exercise, please answer the following questions about how you plan to protect yourself from people, places, and thoughts that may lead you down a path toward relapse.

What will you do when faced with thoughts of going back into old ways of thinking and behaviors?

_____

_____

_____

TAKING CHARGE OF YOUR FUTURE

How will you avoid the people who you know may lead you back into old criminal ways?

_____

_____

_____

What will you do if you cannot avoid these people?

_____

_____

_____

How will you avoid old places that may lead to old patterns of negative behavior?

_____

_____

_____

What will you do if you feel like going back to a negative lifestyle is inevitable, and you think there is nothing to do but go back to old patterns?

_____

_____

_____

MODULE 10

What will you do when you think that no one cares about whether you succeed or fail?

_____

_____

_____

What will you do when you feel like isolating from everyone else and just doing your own thing again?

_____

_____

_____

What will you do when you begin to think you are going to fail?

_____

_____

_____

MODULE 11

Your Support Network

For the most part, we choose the people we associate with. We join groups, make friends, and create families to support one another, as we, too, are supported by these networks and interactions. Truly successful people do not become successful on their own—they utilize and rely on the people around them.

The hardest thing to do for recovering addicts (regardless of your addiction)—and for most people who are struggling to overcome personal adversities—is to pick up the phone and ask for help. We often think we have all the answers or will be fine on our own. Or, we are embarrassed and ashamed. But we were never meant to do this alone!

Ask for help before you need it, and even if you don't think you need it anymore. Ask for it even when you think no one can or wants to help you. Why? Because you are wrong. They can, they want to, and they will.

In this exercise, please answer the following questions about how your support network can aid you in your transition and recovery:

What specific people and/or types of people do you want to surround yourself with?

_____

_____

_____

_____

MODULE 11

What kind of signs do you want your support group to look for in your behavior that may be warning signs that you are about to relapse?

_____

_____

_____

_____

What do you want each person from the list above to do for you if you are in danger of relapsing or going back to detention/prison?

_____

_____

_____

_____

> Drugs, alcohol, and negative thinking will destroy you.
> This is a simple yet undeniable fact.
> Support networks, meetings, and groups are there to help you
> beat these types of influences so that you can succeed in life.

TAKING CHARGE OF YOUR FUTURE

Substance Abuse and Negative Messages Will Destroy Us!

This is a simple yet undeniable fact. Support groups and meetings exist to help people identify and address destructive influences so that they may move on toward living a successful life.

"'Surround yourself with people you want to be like."
Bishop T.D. Jakes

My Support System

Family and Friends:
Whom do you have in your life that can serve as healthy support?

1. _____
2. _____
3. _____
4. _____
5. _____
6. _____
7. _____
8. _____
9. _____
10. _____

Mentors: *A mentor is an experienced and trusted advisor.*
Who are your mentors?

1. _____
2. _____
3. _____

MODULE 11

Support Groups: *People with similar experiences can understand what you're going through.*
What are your support groups?

1. _____
2. _____
3. _____

Spirituality and/or Religion: *These are people and groups that help you stay connected in your search of hope and greater purpose in life.*
What are your spiritual/religious involvements?

1. _____
2. _____

Therapy: *Professional support to help to work through issues and struggles*

1. _____
2. _____
3. _____

Leisure activities and interests: *Provides a break with fun and relaxation, and can help with connecting to others*

1. _____
2. _____
3. _____

MODULE 12

Your Personal-Centered Plan

Person-centered planning (PCP) is a process for selecting and organizing the services and supports that someone may need to live successfully within a community. Most importantly, it is a process directed by the person who receives the support. They make it themselves.

PCP helps a person construct and articulate a vision for the future, consider various paths, engage in decision-making and problem solving, monitor progress, and make needed adjustments in a timely manner. It highlights individual responsibility, including taking appropriate risks. Emergency planning is also often part of the process.

The PCP approach identifies the individual's places, people, fears, strengths/talents, choices, dreams, and SMART GOAL action plans. Unique factors such as culture and language are also taken into account. These elements are included in a highly individualized, unique, written plan for support which will help guide to success.

Person-centered planning should involve every service and support the individual is receiving, such as legal representation, support groups, counseling, and more. These will help define the plan.

Pair up with another participant in your class. Write your name at the top of the next page ("Places"). Hand your book to your partner. You will be interviewing one another for the whole of this exercise and recording one another's answers in the spaces provided. Your mentor or instructor will give you further instructions.

MODULE 12

_____'s places

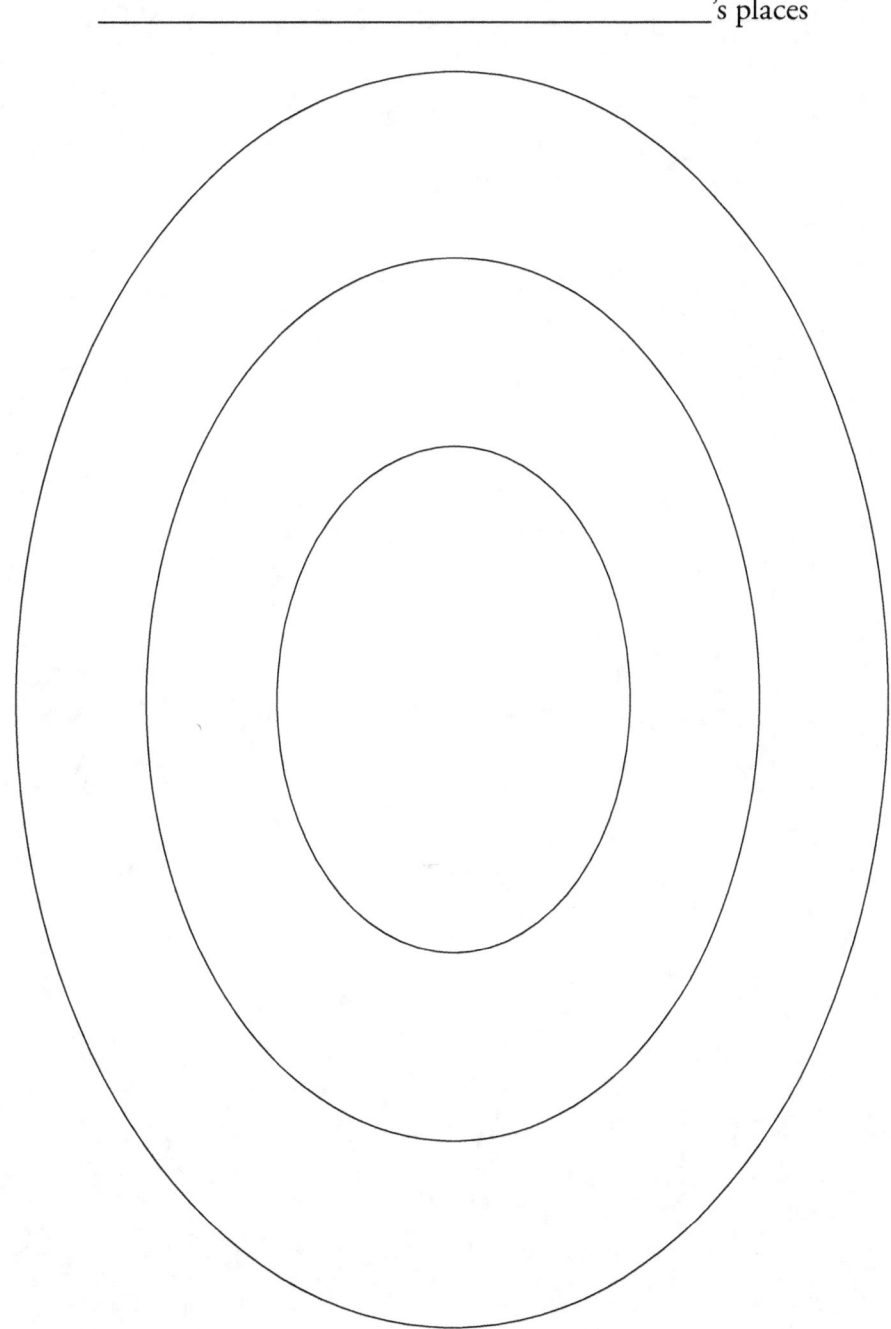

TAKING CHARGE OF YOUR FUTURE

_____'s people

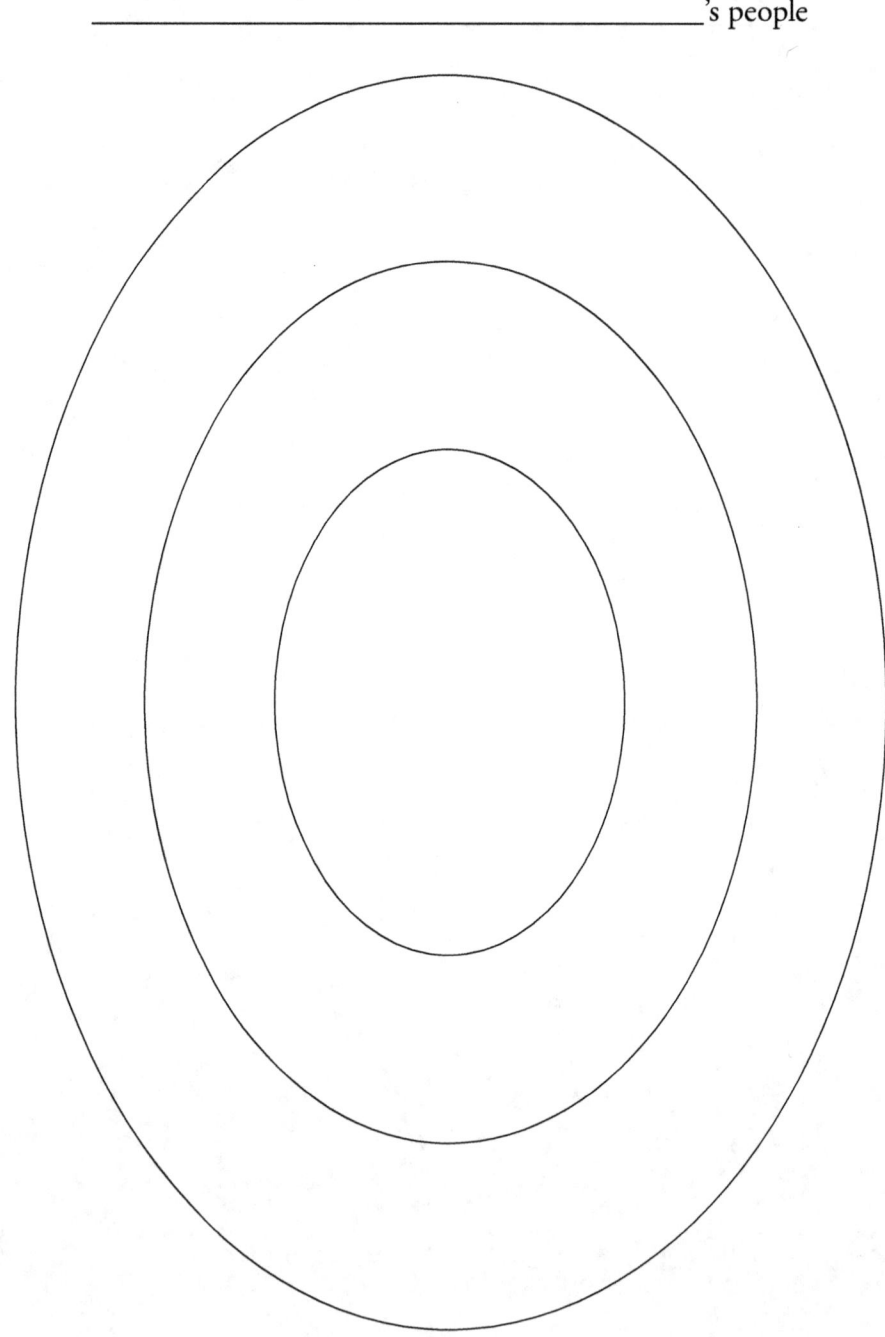

MODULE 12

_____'s fears/worries

- _____
- _____
- _____
- _____
- _____
- _____
- _____
- _____
- _____
- _____
- _____
- _____
- _____
- _____

TAKING CHARGE OF YOUR FUTURE

_____'s strengths/talents

- _____
- _____
- _____
- _____
- _____
- _____
- _____
- _____
- _____
- _____
- _____
- _____
- _____
- _____

MODULE 12

_____'s choices

- _____
- _____
- _____
- _____
- _____
- _____
- _____
- _____
- _____
- _____
- _____
- _____
- _____
- _____

TAKING CHARGE OF YOUR FUTURE

_____'s dreams

- _____
- _____
- _____
- _____
- _____
- _____
- _____
- _____
- _____
- _____
- _____
- _____
- _____
- _____
- _____

MODULE 12

_____'s action plan

What:	Who:	By When:	Status:

TAKING CHARGE OF YOUR FUTURE

_____'s action plan

What:	Who:	By When:	Status:

MODULE 12

_____'s action plan

What:	Who:	By When:	Status:

MODULE 13

Goals, Positive Activities, and Perspective

Having a transition plan is an important part of being ready to transition from any environment into something long-term, positive, and sustainable. It can be hard work and you need to have short- and long-term goals in mind (education, internship, career, income, savings, and homeownership) to become self-sufficient. But all work and no play can make pursuing your desires and life plan a boring and tiresome endeavor.

You must include some "positive activities" while you work toward your goals. Positive activities help to make our journey fun and exciting, and assist you in maintaining a positive outlook and perspective about your future.

In this exercise, please answer the following questions about how you will engage in positive activities as a way of maintaining an upbeat outlook while following your plan:

What practical thing(s) do you want to do when you get settled in your life?

_____

_____

_____

MODULE 13

What do you need to do to have a successful life?

_____

_____

_____

What kinds of things do you want to do for fun once you start moving forward with your life and have the opportunity for leisure activities?

_____

_____

_____

How will you fight boredom and make life feel that it is worth living?

_____

_____

_____

What are your goals for your transition?

_____

_____

_____

TAKING CHARGE OF YOUR FUTURE

What are your *pre*-transition goals?

_____

_____

_____

What actions do you want to define you? What do you want people to see you doing?

_____

_____

_____

What actions do you *not* want to define you? What do you not want people to see you doing?

_____

_____

_____

What do you think a person will tend to do if they define their transition as "too hard"?

_____

_____

_____

MODULE 13

What do you think a person will do if they define their transition as "a stepping stone to greater things"?

_____
_____
_____

Life Changes Going Forward

What was your life like before?

_____
_____
_____

What do you want to change?

_____
_____
_____

What are you going to do to make these changes happen?

_____
_____
_____

TAKING CHARGE OF YOUR FUTURE

What will you do to relax and/or deal with anxiety when stress comes?

_____

_____

_____

What do you need to address about yourself before you transition back into the community?

_____

_____

_____

What old ways of thinking or patterns of behavior could hurt you?

_____

_____

_____

MODULE 14

Dealing with Transittion

Any transition between different environments causes stress—it's a natural reaction. However, this stress can be a trigger that sends us into a relapse. We must learn coping mechanisms to recognize it and handle it in a positive way. This stress does not need to halt all the progress we've made. We can learn to recognize triggers, address them, and continue on our plan.

What concerns do you have about adjusting to your new life after your next transition?

_____

_____

_____

Have you had trouble adapting to new places, people, or situations in the past? What were those situations like?

_____

_____

_____

TAKING CHARGE OF YOUR FUTURE

What have you done before to get through stressful times, or periods of anxiety? Was it successful?

_____

_____

_____

How will you deal with feelings of being numb, lost, anxious, or overwhelmed?

_____

_____

_____

How will you deal with the fear of not being able to find a job, stay off drugs, maintain positive relationships, or any other versions of negative self-talk?

_____

_____

_____

How will you deal with depression, if it arises when expectations are not met and/or you are experiencing the natural pressure of change?

_____

_____

_____

MODULE 14

How will you deal with anger and frustration?

_____

_____

_____

> Believe in yourself and all that you are.
> Know that there is something inside you that is GREATER than any obstacle.
> The most important thing to remember is:
> all transitions eventually end!

It's important to remember that eventually you will get used to your new life; you just need to keep putting one foot in front of the other and moving forward—step by step, day by day.

Know that the emotions you will have before, during, and after transition can be powerful. These feelings need to be dealt with or they will act as a toxin to poison our efforts at success. We need plans for dealing with emotions—especially those we do not think will affect us—because they have a way of blindsiding us. At any point in your transition journey, come back to this section of the manual and read through your responses about dealing with certain emotions as they arise.

MODULE 15

Career Assessment

When I Grow Up...

Even if you have not given too much thought to future career possibilities, you've probably been asked what you want to be when you grow up. You might have even been asked this question many times throughout the course of your adolescence, and your answer may have changed every time!

For this activity, use the space below to either draw or write the first thing you remember wanting to be when you were a child. Have you changed your mind or added other career ideas since then?

Next Steps

Now that you have started to think about careers, what do you do next? Take the career interest survey to kick start your thoughts and inspiration about what direction you'd like to go with future career plans.

Completing the following steps will point you to some general areas where you can explore career possibilities.

Interest Survey

Check off the activities that interest you in each of the boxes. Add each column. Total your answers to discover which career cluster you may want to explore—the areas with the highest number of tallies are where your interests, passions, and talents may lie.

1.

- ❏ Taking care of pets in your neighborhood
- ❏ Transplanting small trees
- ❏ Working in a garden and creating landscapes
- ❏ Nursing sick animals back to health
- ❏ Brushing or grooming dogs, cats and/or horse
- ❏ Hiking and watching wildlife
- ❏ Chopping wood and replanting trees
- ❏ Identifying environmental hazards and sick/dying plants

Total checks _____

2.

- ❏ Repairing small appliances
- ❏ Painting houses or buildings
- ❏ Using tools to make household repairs
- ❏ Cutting and shaping wood to build structures
- ❏ Volunteering for Habitat for Humanity
- ❏ Drawing floor plans
- ❏ Building simple circuit boards
- ❏ Laying brick or cinder block
- ❏ Landscaping and planting flower gardens

Total checks _____

3.

- ❏ Performing (music, drama, or dance for an audience
- ❏ Creating graphic designs on a computer
- ❏ Creating an original video or film
- ❏ Sketching or painting pictures
- ❏ Taking photographs
- ❏ Writing poems, stories, or plays
- ❏ Making jewelry, sculptures, ceramics, or stained glass
- ❏ Designing a newspaper layout
- ❏ Being an announcer for an amateur radio station

Total checks _____

4.

- ❏ Using a cash register
- ❏ Typing minutes of a meeting
- ❏ Filing or sorting mail or other papers
- ❏ Running your own business
- ❏ Developing web pages and creating layouts using desktop publishing
- ❏ Managing tasks for a group
- ❏ Preparing reports and analyzing data
- ❏ Typing documents for other people
- ❏ Volunteering to answer phones

Total checks _____

TAKING CHARGE OF YOUR FUTURE

5.

- ❏ Working as a kids' camp counselor or volunteer
- ❏ Tutoring children or students
- ❏ Reading to elementary school students
- ❏ Giving instructions for/or directing a play
- ❏ Babysitting young children
- ❏ Organizing and shelving library books
- ❏ Peer counseling or mediation
- ❏ Helping at Special Olympics events
- ❏ Working at an after-school program

Total checks _____

6.

- ❏ Planning a mock stock market game
- ❏ Investing money and studying investments
- ❏ Balancing a checkbook
- ❏ Opening a savings/checking account
- ❏ Being a treasurer for a club
- ❏ Organizing a fundraiser
- ❏ Collecting money for a school or community event
- ❏ Developing a budget
- ❏ Using spreadsheets and financial computer programs

Total checks _____

7.

- ❏ Campaigning for a political candidate
- ❏ Making political speeches
- ❏ Volunteering as an urban planning committee member
- ❏ Running for class office
- ❏ Planning and preparing budgets
- ❏ Participating in a debate
- ❏ olunteering as a legislative aide
- ❏ Learning and speaking a foreign language
- ❏ Researching and writing grants

Total checks _____

8.

- ❏ Taking care of a sick relative
- ❏ Watching doctor/hospital shows on TV
- ❏ Learning first aid and CPR
- ❏ Volunteering at a retirement home
- ❏ Volunteering as a hospital aide
- ❏ Using a stethoscope to listen to someone's heart
- ❏ Identifying human body parts from a diagram
- ❏ Bandaging sports injuries with a trainer's help
- ❏ Assisting persons in wheelchairs with daily tasks

Total checks _____

9.

- ❏ Working in a restaurant
- ❏ Planning vacations and other events
- ❏ Cooking, baking, and serving meals
- ❏ Participating in sports or recreation activities
- ❏ Being a lifeguard
- ❏ Catering an event
- ❏ Working at a concession stand
- ❏ Exercising and working out
- ❏ Officiating a sports event

Total checks _____

10.

- ❏ Making a family menu
- ❏ Working with the elderly
- ❏ Working at a shelter
- ❏ Shopping, comparing prices and consumer goods
- ❏ Listening and helping friends with problems
- ❏ Participating in youth groups or community groups
- ❏ Working as a dietician's aide
- ❏ Volunteering at a retirement home
- ❏ Volunteering to be a Big Brother/Big Sister

Total checks _____

11.

- ❏ Developing software programs
- ❏ Building computers
- ❏ Playing video games
- ❏ Surfing the internet
- ❏ Learning how to configure operating systems
- ❏ Installing software
- ❏ Learning how to assemble computer hardware
- ❏ Playing with electronic gadgets
- ❏ Designing video games

Total checks _____

12.

- ❏ Reading mystery novels
- ❏ Listening to a police scanner
- ❏ Watching mystery movies or courtroom dramas
- ❏ Playing "Clue "or other mystery board games
- ❏ Volunteering in a lawyer's office
- ❏ Following court cases in the news
- ❏ Participating in EMT training
- ❏ Volunteering to search for missing pets or persons
- ❏ Participating in search and rescue training

Total checks _____

13.

- ❏ Welding or working with metals
- ❏ Repairing and upholstering furniture
- ❏ Creating wood carvings
- ❏ Taking machine shop classes
- ❏ Making belts or other leather goods
- ❏ Operating a printing press
- ❏ Installing and repairing home electronics
- ❏ Sewing, weaving, knitting, or other needlework
- ❏ Building cabinets, shelves, and other woodworking

Total checks _____

14.

- ❏ Cutting and styling hair
- ❏ Selling products for a school fundraiser
- ❏ Taking tours of new houses for sale
- ❏ Designing of modeling clothes
- ❏ Giving people advice on products they should buy
- ❏ Decorating your house and rearranging your furniture
- ❏ Planning and having a yard sale
- ❏ Arranging and selling flowers
- ❏ Fixing watches and clocks

Total checks _____

15.

- ❏ Visiting science museums
- ❏ Designing experiments
- ❏ Exploring caves and collecting rocks
- ❏ Watching the weather and tracking storms
- ❏ Using a computer to solve math problems and equations.
- ❏ Identifying plants, animals, and/or marine life
- ❏ Developing solution to environmental problems
- ❏ Building model aircraft, boats, and trains
- ❏ Learning about different cultures

Total checks _____

16.

- ❏ Flying airplanes
- ❏ Repairing vehicles, bikes, and engines
- ❏ Working in a warehouse or taking inventory
- ❏ Operating motorized machines or equipment
- ❏ Visiting space camps
- ❏ Building and reaping boats
- ❏ Operating a CB or ham radio
- ❏ Reading mechanical and automotive magazines
- ❏ Having a paper route

Total checks _____

MODULE 15

Interest Survey Totals

Count the check marks in each section and place the total in the corresponding box below:

1. Agriculture, Food, & Natural Resources _____	2. Architecture & Construction _____	3. Arts, Audio/Visual Technology, & Communications _____	4. Business Management & Administration _____
5. Education & Training _____	6. Finance _____	7. Government & Public Administration _____	8. Health Science _____
9. Hospitality & Tourism _____	10. Human Services _____	11. Information Technology _____	12. Law, Public Safety, Corrections, & Security _____
13. Manufacturing _____	14. Marketing _____	15. Science, Technology, Engineering, & Math _____	16. Transportation, Distribution & Logistics _____

My Top Three Interest Areas:

1. _____ 2. _____ 3. _____

As you can see, the interest survey is divided into 16 groups, and each group is a career cluster. Career clusters place similar occupations in groups, and these clusters help you narrow down the thousands of career options in the world to a general area of interest. This will give you a bit of a "jumping off" point. The clusters connect what you learn in school to the skills and knowledge you need in the real world. Some careers are placed in more than one cluster.

MODULE 16

Financial Management/Budgeting

How good are you at managing your money? Creating a budget and staying within your budget will be one of the most important aspects of your transition. To manage your money, you need to know exactly how much money you have (and make sure you never spend more than you have coming in!).

In the two columns below, we will look at your income and expenses both presently and in the future. Your instructor can help you fill in the blanks if you are unsure of the actual amounts.

Income		Expenses	
Wages, Salaries, Tips	$ _____	Housing	$ _____
Alimony	$ _____	Utilities	$ _____
Child Support	$ _____	Food	$ _____
TANF	$ _____	Personal Care	$ _____
WIC	$ _____	Clothing	$ _____
Food Stamps	$ _____	Phone	$ _____
SSI	$ _____	Transportation (Car)	$ _____
SSDI	$ _____	Gas	$ _____
Unemployment	$ _____	Insurance	$ _____
Pension/Annuities	$ _____	Payment	$ _____

TAKING CHARGE OF YOUR FUTURE

VA Benefits	$ _____	Transportation (Bus)	$ _____
General Relief Assist.	$ _____	Laundry	$ _____
Dividend Income	$ _____	Child Support	$ _____
Business (Partner)	$ _____	Child Care	$ _____
Capital Gain	$ _____	LFO's/Debt	$ _____
Other Misc. Income	$ _____	Misc. (Credit Card)	$ _____
		Misc.	$ _____
Total Monthly Income	$ _____	**Total Expenses**	$ _____

Calculate Disposable Income

Monthly Income $ _____ Monthly Expenses $ _____ = Disposable Income $ _____

MODULE 17

Developing Your Plan

As mentioned before, the individualized transition plan is a pathway that will help you to achieve the objectives and goals you associate with your future life and success. No successful business, person, or organization can achieve success without having a plan of action outlining how they are going to achieve their goals. Once you take the time to make your customized plan, you will be able to reference it in the days, months, and even months ahead as you make progress and adapt to your new environment(s).

In this exercise, please use the following questions below as a guideline for helping you develop your Personal Plan.

Introduction: Your introduction should be a summary of your short- and long-term plans, and where you see yourself 12 months from now. In reviewing your introduction, the reader should be able to see a well-defined pathway for how you intend to achieve your goals.

Your plan should start from your day of transition, covering the first three days, 30 days, 60 days, and 90 days. Your introduction should present a summary of how you plan to sustain yourself and what support network (e.g., community, family, groups) and community resources you need in order to achieve your desired goals. Your answers from Module 1 ("Who Am I?"), your PCP, and the questions in this module can help you with your introductory statement.

_____

_____

_____

___

___

___

___

___

___

___

___

Support System (Network): Your support system is made up of groups of people (i.e., friends, extended family, colleagues and/or professionals) that you can count on for help when you need it. These are the individuals you feel comfortable going to for information and encouragement when you need to make informed decisions.

Who are some of these people/systems in your life?

___

___

___

___

MODULE 17

Family Support: Are your family members people you can really count on? You only want to list all the biological and extended family members that you can count on to be there for you. These are the family members who encourage and help you make informed decisions that are in your best interests.

_____

_____

_____

_____

_____

_____

Who are some of these people/networks in your life?

_____

_____

_____

_____

_____

_____

Housing: Is your housing secure? What are your housing options (e.g., homeless shelter, community-based transitional housing program, living with family and/or friends, clean and sober house)? Do you have access to a permanent home or apartment? List three housing options that will be available to you as you transition:

_____

_____

_____

_____

_____

_____

Education: Please list all certificates, GEDs, diplomas, and/or degrees that you have obtained.

_____

_____

_____

_____

_____

_____

MODULE 17

Employment History: List your previous employment history. Where have you worked? In addition, please list any career opportunities you will have as you transition.

_____

_____

_____

_____

_____

_____

Finances and Financial Support: Make a list of your first-line financial support once you are released (e.g., family, friends, DSHS, SSI assistance).

_____

_____

_____

_____

_____

_____

TAKING CHARGE OF YOUR FUTURE

Hobbies and Interests: Make a list of the hobbies and relaxing activities that you will be involved in, once released.

_____

_____

_____

_____

_____

_____

Motivation: List some of the motivational activities that you will be engaged in or involved with following your release (support groups, clubs, religious groups and classes, etc.).

_____

_____

_____

_____

_____

_____

MODULE 17

Real Talk to Encourage Change: Use this section to list some of the pro-social people you will be involved with who not be afraid to have real conversations with you to continue the process of fostering change and growth following your release:

_____

_____

_____

_____

_____

_____

MODULE 18

Your 30-Day Goals

In order for you to maximize your plan, you need to be strategic with your time and the people you are spending time with.

In this exercise, please list all the activities, events, achievements, and milestones that you would like to accomplish within the first 30 days of your transition. Try to keep it simple!

My goals for the first 30 days of my transition:

1. _____
2. _____
3. _____
4. _____
5. _____
6. _____
7. _____
8. _____

MODULE 18

9. _____

10. _____

11. _____

12. _____

13. _____

14. _____

15. _____

16. _____

17. _____

18. _____

19. _____

20. _____

MODULE 19

Your Six-Month Goals

By the time you reach the six-month mark, you need to start defining your plan and become more strategic with identifying all the "what/why/where/when/how" of your plan.

In this exercise, identify below your "What?" (your desire goal), your "Why?" (did you choose this goal), your "Where?" (do go to accomplish this goal), your "When?" (are you going to start), and your "How?" (will you complete this goal).

Six months after transition I see myself as:

What: _____

_____

Why: _____

_____

_____

Where: _____

_____

_____

MODULE 19

When: _____

_____

_____

How: _____

_____

_____

Resources needed: _____

_____

_____

MODULE 20

Your One-Year Goals

In this exercise, answer the question to identify where you would like to be by the end of the first year of your plan. What changes would you like to see in yourself in your attitude and behavior? What about your employment or family situations?

One year after transition I see myself:

Where: _____

_____

What: _____

_____

_____

Why: _____

_____

_____

MODULE 20

When: _____

_____

_____

How: _____

_____

_____

Resources needed: _____

_____

_____

MODULE 21

Your Three-Year Goals

In this exercise, answer the questions to identify where you would like to be by the end of the third year of your plan. How would you like to see yourself and your lifestyle change beyond the immediate future? How do you see your family? Your career?

Three years after transition, I see myself:

Where: _____

_____

What: _____

_____

_____

_____

Why: _____

_____

_____

MODULE 21

When: _____

_____

_____

How: _____

_____

_____

Resources needed: _____

_____

_____

CONCLUSION

Well done on completing this course. You are now much better equipped to truly "take charge of your future!"

As a reminder, it's important to acknowledge that part of being able to move forward is the ability to look back at where you have come from. This workbook was created to be a self-help journey to understanding yourself on a deep and authentic level. In Module 2, we asked you to identify in your own words how you see yourself.

In this exercise, we are asking the same questions we asked in Module 2, as a way of introducing you to the power of the change, growth, and confidence that has increased since you started this journey. Now, you are connected to the power of self-awareness through developing your Personalized Smart Goals Plan. Let's see how your thinking and outlook have changed since undertaking this course.

Re-asking the Question: *Who Am I?*

What kind of person were you before your current situation?

_____

_____

What kind of person are you today?

_____

_____

TAKING CHARGE OF YOUR FUTURE

What kind of person do you want to be?

_____

_____

How do you want to be remembered?

_____

_____

What kind of impact would you like to make on the world? On your family and community?

_____

_____

What words of advice would you give to your younger self, based on what you've learned?

_____

_____

IT'S TIME TO TAKE CHARGE OF YOUR FUTURE!

ABOUT THE AUTHORS

Gerald Bradford was born and raised in Seattle, Washington, and attended Garfield High School and the University of Washington.

Upon college graduation, Gerald intended on going to law school, but instead fell in love with working with people. He discovered he was passionate about helping individuals move forward with their lives.

After serving with the King County Juvenile Detention Center as an employment counselor, Gerald began working as a counselor with gang members in South Seattle and the Central District. Since then, he's been serving the community in a variety of different ways as a mentor, coach, counselor, uncle, brother, and friend.

In 2005, Gerald began working in re-entry service for the King County Jail—counseling men and women on continuing their education, finding a career, and settling into a positive and productive lifestyle after incarceration. For over 15 years, he has been working with adult populations and was the first ever Education and Employment Navigator hired by the State of Washington.

Gerald currently works as the Re-Entry Manager at Renton Technical College and is a founding member of Fresh Start Professional Services and Seattle Peace and Safety Initiative. He is currently serving as the Vice President of the Central District Preservation Authority (CDCPDA).

Terrence L. Morgan is the CEO and Co-Founder of Fresh Start Professional Services. Born and raised in Seattle, Terrence attended and graduated from Seattle Public Schools and received his Associate degree from Pierce College.

Terrence has dedicated his life to educating and assisting individuals impacted by the criminal justice system and is passionate about preparing them for their return into the community and navigating the multiple systems at play. For the last decade, Terrence has worked in the community service field, focusing on the needs of people coming out of prisons, jails, homelessness, family reunification, and domestic violence. Terrence has partnered with the YMCA, Juvenile Justice, Department of Corrections (DOC), and Greenhill High School.

Terrence has a vision to help bring equality to people of color and the BIPOC communities through empowerment, building community, education, career-based employment, and supporting community businesses. His experience as co-author of *Taking Charge of Your Future*, which was first offered to the Washington State DOC population under a different title for a period of five years—along with his skills in system navigation and community resources allocation—earned him a leadership position with the Urban League of Metropolitan Seattle, which in turn led to a position as the Workforce Development Program Manager overseeing their Career Bridge Program. He is currently working as a Lead Case Manager for Adonai Employment and Counseling, serving King, Snohomish, and Pierce Counties in Washington State.

Franklyn R. Smith is well-known for his work of more than 15 years in developing productive pathways for adults in transition to obtain the essential supports necessary to experience a successful transition from homelessness, incarceration, and treatment programs (e.g., housing, food, clothing, employment, and pro-social). He was born and raised in Seattle, WA, graduated from Seattle Public Schools, and holds a degree in Business/Accounting with certificates in Supervisory Management, Leadership, Advance Correction Case Management, Workforce Development, WA/DBHA Peer Support Counseling, and Credible Messenger Trainings.

Franklyn is currently the Director of Community Resources at Freedom Project WA and Co-Founder of Fresh Start Professional Service (NPPSC) in Seattle, WA. In 2014, Franklyn developed a Supportive Transitional Re-Entry Model that was presented to the BJA/WA-DOC Second Chance Re-Entry Pilot Project Steering Committee. In 2015, he was the first formerly justice-involved individual to be hired by the WA/DOC as a Community Resources Program Manager and Correction Specialist 3/Re-Entry Navigator. He is also the co-creator of Sober Solutions Transitional Housing LLC, and has consulted in developing Divinity, RAZ Community Services and several other transitional housing programs.

To reach the authors, or for more information, contact:
www.freshstartps.org

www.ingramcontent.com/pod-product-compliance
Lightning Source LLC
Chambersburg PA
CBHW081754100526
44592CB00015B/2430